Quantum e-motions

Fernanda Loveland

BookLeaf
Publishing

India | USA | UK

Presentation by *BookLeaf Publishing*

Web: www.bookleafpub.com

E-mail: info@bookleafpub.com

ISBN: 9789358316940

First edition 2023

*To all of those who have a vision. Your light
guides you.*

ACKNOWLEDGEMENT

To my mom for her youthful heart and confident love.
To my Papa Ricardo for his strength and eternal presence.
To my Mama Leyta for showing me the infinite power of faith.

PREFACE

The enduring task of writting a book came to me as fast as a comet and as light as thin air. One day, I decided to adopt the habit of writing, fueled by the objective of gaining control over the indomable: my emotions. At the time, these sensations where blurry and diluted, free spirited as watercolors. Gradually, the novelty of expressing myself through the infinite shading of words, provided my feelings with the ideal containers. My feelings adopted the new space provided for them and grew in detail and depth. This book represents the final look at the canvas where my emotions are the paint. Blended by a brush called passion to form these artful dance called poetry.

Big loop

Every idea
A big bang
An initial collision
Eruption at the center of our soul

With its authentic shine
Deserving the same
weight and gravity
As the original Big Bang
That created it all
Eternal combustion
In the loop of creation

Your place of origin
Can be traced to the heart-mind dance
when the orbits of these two celestial organs
coincide
When this happens, a shining spark
The newborn idea arises
Tingling
Words home the idea
Developing it
Expanding its power
Until the idea is ready
To be shared

Fill the space with its light
The idea, now a star
Shines autonomous
Immortalized energy

Foggy

And I saw the grey sky
And It felt welcoming
Neutral
Present
Stagnant
Consistent
Like a slightly tinted canvas
Awaiting with open arms
For the day to be whatever it wants to be
Will it be a happy day?
It can be
But the humble canvas
Accepts all shades of emotions
Including gray
Unpretentiously creative
Valuable because of its honesty
The foggy day allows us to be
Our authentic, sometimes gloomy, self.

Madam Moon

If what I feel is an ocean
I want to taste every drop
Dive into every wave
Touch, explore, feel
submerge into
The deepest caves.
Consumed by thirst
But also satiety
Of something I've never felt
But at the same time so familiar
Blue ocean Moon
Moon that watches me
You witness my passion
Container of this fuel
Directing it into the fire
in which it will consume
Eternally

Emerald

5

Such was the color of the water
Of the ocean that has accompanied me
During the last two years
In the beginning
As I took that first walk on your shore
Allured by the solitude of your sands
Captivated by the imposing pier
Immersed in your breeze
Naive and successful
Exploring
The new landscape
That would be the set place
a discovery of myself
On the emerald coast

A poem inspired by kid cudi

If you can do what you imagine
Then what is imagination
To you
Weight of Creation
You can create anything
With courage
Stand up straight
My life artisan
Side by side
Proud of your gold seeds
You, author of creation
The I
As patient as I nurtured them
As brave as I trusted their expansion
Same intensity
I'm one with my idea

Day time dramatist

Does true love even exist?
More than decoration,
Beautifully frugal
More than narrative,
Pleasurably fictional
More than syntax
A lover of semantics

Does this all-encompassing accesible and
universal- must have the color red for sure- love,
exist?
Are the other individuals
Genuinely concerned
Or am I a character
That builds
Enhances
Enriches
Their life story
Will the feeling
Endure more than one chapter?
Or will it linger,
Slowly extinguished
Sudden premise
Am I the director
That orchestrated

All this theatrical
Downfall, I question
Hoping
with all this red velvet heart
That this play
Called love
Opens its curtains once again.

Little life surprises

And suddenly
I stop
The continuous unfolding
Of the current activity
I'm surprised
By the breeze
At the top of the hill
The moment
At its peak
Identity and experience
Become one
My eyes glance
At a bluish light
Blue as mourning
Wanting to feel this whole for eternity
But also blue tinted of hope
Impermanence
Shining light on
moments of sweet ecstasy
That arise
As ordinary life surprises

I know how passionate you are

I feel it with every touch
Your inner fire
Allowing its signs
To emerge to the surface
And in some moments
Flames of that fire arise
Unhinged
Uncontained
Unraveled
And I can feel
The intensity of your insides
For a split second
Oh, all of your wilderness
So tangible, our surfaces one
My light shines only in your domain

Shoreline

Synchronized
We met on a humble day
Inconspicuous moment
Birthed
Extraordinary connection
And such was the surprise
When hand in hand
We witnessed our chaos
I found in you a comrade
A reflection of my wildest side
A courageous calling
A mind that reflected mine
And a heart that understood my ache
There are few things
Refreshing like the fresh
ocean water
Sharing the shore
Our feet
Deep in this bond
warm as a heartfelt smile
brave as a word of courage
You have been that and more
Soulsister

Shine

What is love
More than the deep hope
Of seeing the light
Of the beloved soul
Shine
You changed my world
On a Sunnv February Sunday
My eyes met your smile
The ones I had seen days prior
Limited by the rigidity of pixels

Boundless now
Admiring it
Bright in front of me

deep inside i knew
That something had forever changed
Admiring the shine
Of your loving smile
I couldn't conceive how until that day
I had been living restfully
Ignorantly
blinded to the purest of joys
Finally, when I saw your smile
Deep inside I knew
It was the beginning
Of our journey

Loving vessel

Love your body
A phrase so usual
That it's meaning
Has torn mundane
When you hear someone
Directing these words
As bullets towards you
Love your body
A phrase so ambiguous
Pretentious
How do you even start?
What is the first
Building block
To dismantle the walls we have built
Around our body
This solo mission
Has one objective
Dismantling
Brick by brick
The feeling of rejection
To our life house
Catered to us
On a bizarre perspective
Perhaps our initial sense of
Rejection

To our vessels
Is an innate expression
 of the initial shock
Our spirits
 Contained into flesh
The unfamiliarity
That comes in the novelty of life itself
Reclaiming the praise
To the fragility of our body
Allow us to accept
As there is no ideal life
There isn't an ideal body
Directing our love
Towards all of our own quirky bits
Transforms rejection into love
Forming a new wall
Rather than separation
Support, sustain and sympathy
For our
Human life vessels.

Touch

I just want to be touched
To feel your lingering
Fingers
Trace a path around my sacred hidden
Spots
I want to feel the touch
Undisturbed
For a while
For an everlasting moment
For your caresses to not have a byproduct
For the love emerging out of your hands
To not be misguided
By what our tormented minds desire
But aligned
By what our hearts crave

Contained in the catacombs
of my soul

I observe my passionate nature
But i pledge guilty of denying it in everyday life
the existence
of this being
This essence i have contained, far away

Listen to me, it begs
Answer me, it demans
Let me out, it suplicates

Trembling at the idea of revealing myself

despite being hidden,
on my obscure inhibitions
It will live forever
remembering the light
and taking a peak
every now and then

I want to feel us

discover the most hidden part of our souls,
share the vortex of our psyche

memories, anecdotes, epiphanies and
observations
Our own scientific method of the world
I want to feel that my soul connects with yours
in a transcendental way.
cleared of superficial blur,
I want to feel my soul lost in yours.

Unintentional glance

My eyes dance around
foolishly taking
An unintentional glance
Suddenly
a sweet splendor
makes them hostage

My reason states
that, OBJECTIVELY
your eyes aren't directed at me
More than rejected
it's expected
As we don't have a relational connection.

You are your node and I am mine

There is no link to unite us

no direct relationship

but in a bridge between the fictional and real
world

I heard your laugh and saw your smile
A light so ordinarily sublime

Said laughter was not caused by me
neither directed at my eyes
But it trapped me organically
How excentric
the organic connection

of neurons

of synapses

objective, clear, and concise

There was nothing before nor there be (who
knows) anything after
More than this fragment
between you and i
Discretely bonded

human android

After elevating myself
through multiple perspectives
High flying
Saw my avatar
Saw my designated divine android
Saw myself
Procuring
With all of the capacity
That I've witnessed
To trust the mission given
Safeguarding
The expanding perspective
After seeing
With my own two eyes
Infinity
I will identify with my avatar
Refraining pride from
Taking over
My simple human
Mundane problems
I will identify with my avatar
This soft tissued free vessel I was given
self compassion
Assessing my trivialities
One by one,

Humble human
Universally conscious
Individually identified
Eternally capable
Apprentice of the moment

Bello uomo

Grazie Bello Uomo
Thank you for making my dreams come true
Staring into your eyes
Deeply
Observing the passionate darkness of your
pupils
I wonder
What are the contents of your dreams
What makes your soul ignite
In my case,
A while ago
I dreamed of you

Now,
A fraction
A tiny fraction of a light year later
we are sitting on a boat
Your hand is on my leg
You are at my side
Serene
You are the source of love
That flows like a waterfall
And it continues to flow
Passing through rocks and deposits
Persevering

serene and
flowing

we are sitting on a boat

Your hand on my leg
And everything around me
Of the most delicate shade of light
my eyes have never
witnessed
Nonetheless
The music that my ears listen to
The light that my eyes capture
The wine that my mouth tastes
Tortellini,
Aperol spritz
Limincello
Futile delicacies

For the first time in my life equation,
No sensation
compares to seeing you
Resembles having you
Equals loving you

Warrior

Initial act of courage
Crossing the threshold
Believing
You are the warrior of fear
Suitor of autonomy
Artisan of your life
I implore you
Standing tall
Hold your sword
And pridefully
Confront your fears

Cavern

Here I go again
Sun shimmering
Gifting me
Bright courage
Stiffens these timorous feet
I stand now firmly
On top of the cavernous place

I gaze down
My eyes firm, the only spectators
Abyss in front of me
Of surprising depth
Sunken area
Left by your absence
On the once beautiful soil
In my Loveland

Sitting now
In my own solitude
Words become clear
Reflections of the feeling
one doesn't realize
the cave's deepness
Until the heartfelt space
Is left empty
When one gazes down
From far, far away

Songbird

When will my time
To cease to be careless
Come upon?
When will the bells
Indicate with a chime
The starting line
My initiation
In the race of meaning
When will I stop
Dancing beautifully
Swirling Between
Clouds of ideas
Like a flying bird
when will I
Become an eagle
Master of vision
Driven by
Sagacious will
Choosing to commit
And devour
my goal

Infinity Roses

Infinity roses
A delicate harmony
Of flawlessly placed petals
Bursting Carmine
Contrasting burgundy shadows
A passionate blend

Such an ardent gift
Took place on a sunny June evening
with a calm stance
You sat and unraveled the vessel
That suppressed them
Methodically, patiently, calmly
As each an every action that you endure

Their h raceful petals now free
You revealed expectantly
As if their innate beauty
Had to be perceived by my eyes
To be consummated

As the perpetual moment
Was being born
my eyes caught yours

Holding each other as two dancing partners
Aware of each others movements
excited and piercing stares
A sensuous search
In each others eyes
For a sign of recognition

That June evening
As I experienced
Your beloved intention
To give a start to our path
Our journey together
like a passenger in an airplane
Waiting for the plane to take off
Patiently expecting what is to come
Never would I had imagined
The heights our love would reach
The firm foundation it would form
The undiscovered lands it would conquer
All emerged from the love
In this imperishable roses